STEP-BY-STEP

TABLE

DECORATING

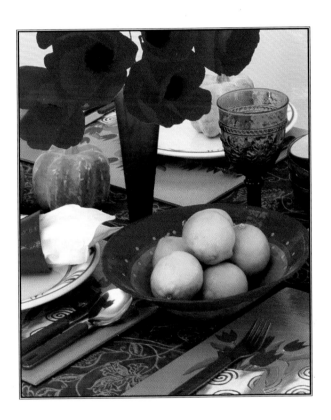

Adams Media Corporation
Holbrook, Massachusetts

STEP-BY-STEP

TABLE
DECORATING

ELAINE LEVITTE

Contents

INTRODUCTION

The decorated table

The success of a meal relies on more than just good food. A beautifully set table goes a long way to creating the right ambience for a truly memorable meal. And there is no need to spend a fortune on the finest linen, china and cut-

lery. Of course, these objects are great decorating aids, but this book is dedicated to those of you who enjoy the challenge of doing it yourself. In the following chapters you will learn how easy it is to create a range of exciting settings with hand-crafted objects, and without any special skills.

There are very few rules when it comes to table decorating, and many of these can be broken. Those that can't be are adhered to mainly for practical reasons. For example, a centerpiece should be either low enough to see over or elevated on a support that will not obstruct the view across the table.

Another consideration is lighting. As romantic as dinner by candlelight may sound, it is still important to be able to see what you are eating and drinking, so make sure that you either use enough candles or supplement the candlelight with another light source. On the other hand, bright, direct light may be appropriate for a regular family dinner, but it is unlikely to help create that special atmosphere you want when entertaining.

Although some celebrations still call for formal table settings, these tend to be the exception rather than the rule. The current trend favors a far more casual approach to dining, and correspondingly informal settings reflect this trend. Who dictated that knives, forks and spoons must be laid out like soldiers on either side of a dinner plate? And does it really matter if the side plate is placed above the dinner plate rather than on its left? Be bold and lend a lighthearted approach to your table settings. Try tying the cutlery in a bundle with a beautiful piece of ribbon and placing it on the dinner plate. Or go for the eclectic look with an interesting selection of mismatched china, cutlery and glassware. If you prefer to play it safe, stick to basic white plates that can be dressed up or down to suit the occasion. An all-white table setting with a crisply starched cloth and napkins will always look elegant, but if you prefer, you could introduce brightly colored or patterned accessories such as a hand-painted cloth, checked napkins or a vase of gay spring flowers.

Don't wait for a special occasion before putting some basic table-decorating ideas into practice. A little bit of effort can turn an ordinary meal into a memorable one — then just wait for the compliments to roll in!

CHAPTER ONE

Bright for breakfast

Start the day on a bright note at a table set with a colorful assortment of china and glassware on a special hand-stenciled cloth. Coordinating napkins together with a croissant tray and an informal floral arrangement complete the picture.

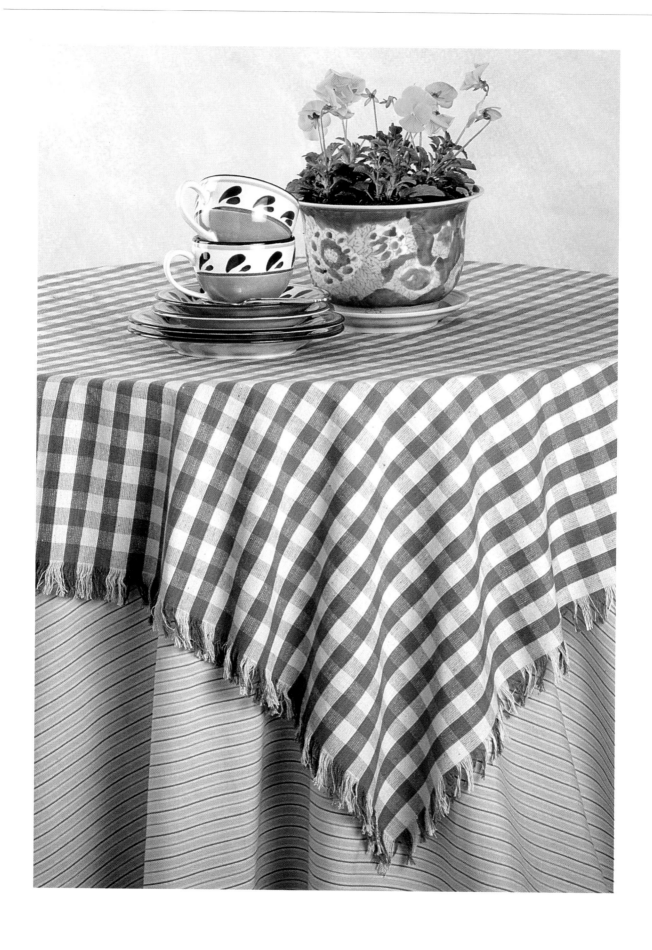

The basic cloth

Making a plain tablecloth is simplicity itself, no matter what the shape or size of your table.
The cloth can be decorated in a variety of ways to suit your tastes and needs.

MATERIALS & EQUIPMENT

- ◆ Cotton fabric (quantity will depend on the size of the table — see STEP 1)
- ◆ Sewing thread to match the fabric
- ◆ Tape measure
- ◆ Scissors

FOR A ROUND CLOTH YOU WILL ALSO NEED:

- ◆ A push pin
- ◆ A length of string
- ◆ A pencil
- ◆ Brown paper or newsprint (optional)

DIAGRAM 1

SQUARE OR RECTANGULAR CLOTH

1. *Measure the length and width of the top of the table and add 24 inches to each measurement. This includes 2 inches for the hems, and will give the cloth a 10-inch drop all around.*

2. *Cut out the required shape to the calculated size, along the grain of the fabric. Turn in the edges twice by 1 inch to form a neat hem. Stitch the hem down along all four edges.*

ROUND CLOTH

1. *Measure the diameter of the tabletop. Add 24 inches to this measurement — this allows for a 2-inch hem all around and a 10-inch drop.*

2. *Cut out a square of fabric with sides as long as the total diameter calculated above. If the fabric is not wide enough, seams will be necessary. Instead of one seam down the center, join an extra strip of fabric to either side of a central panel, keeping the side panels equal widths (DIAGRAM 1).*

3. *Fold the fabric in quarters. Work on a flat surface into which you can insert a pushpin, and do so at the corner of the folded square which is the center of the piece of fabric (DIAGRAM 2). Tie a length of string to the pin and attach a pencil to the other end of the string so that the point of the pencil is on the opposite edge of the folded square. Holding the pencil upright, draw a quarter circle on the fabric by carefully moving the pencil across from corner to corner (DIAGRAM 2). Cut along the line through all four layers of fabric. If you prefer, you can use this method to make a paper pattern before cutting the fabric.*

4. *Machine- or hand-stitch a 2-inch hem all round.*

DIAGRAM 2

The painted cloth

Fabric painting is simple and fun. Draw inspiration from a favorite plate or mug with a clearly defined design that is easy to duplicate. You may feel confident enough to paint your fabric freehand, but easy-to-cut stencils will ensure uniformity of design while maintaining a hand-crafted look.

MATERIALS & EQUIPMENT

- Plain tablecloth made as described on PAGE 11
- Fabric paints in the colors of your choice
- Tracing paper
- Pencil
- Stencil card or clear acetate film
- Fine-tipped permanent marker (if using acetate film)
- Sharp craft knife
- Masking tape
- Sponge
- Paper towel or newspaper
- Iron

1. *Draw or trace your chosen design and use a photocopier to enlarge it to the desired size. If the design source, (for example, a plate) can be placed straight onto a photocopier, this will make the job much easier.*

2. *A separate stencil is required for each color of the design. Clear acetate film will allow you to trace directly off your artwork with a permanent marker. If you are using an opaque stencil card, trace the outline of each color off the artwork separately and transfer it onto the stencil card. Make sure that each piece of card or acetate is at least 4 inches bigger than your design in width and length.*

3. *Using a craft knife, carefully cut out the stencils for each color from the sheets of acetate or card (PHOTO 1).*

4. *Position the first stencil on the cloth and secure it with masking tape. Cut a piece of sponge that is easy to grip with your fingertips.*

5. *Dip the sponge in the paint and daub off any excess paint on a piece of paper towel or newspaper — very little paint is required and the sponge should be as dry as possible to prevent "bleeding" under the edges of the stencil. Apply the paint to the cut-out area of the stencil with a daubing motion* (PHOTO 2). *Don't worry if the paint looks blotchy when wet — it is a very forgiving medium and*

dries to a subtle finish. In any case, irregularities in color intensity create interesting results.

6. *Carefully remove the stencil and reposition it to repeat the design. As you will need to use very little paint, it will dry very quickly and you can proceed with your next color almost immediately. To do this, superimpose your second*

stencil over the dry painted area and sponge on the second color with another sponge (PHOTO 3). *Repeat this process until all colors are applied.*

7. *To fix the paint, iron on the reverse side of the cloth at the maximum temperature suggested for the material, going over each stenciled area for about three minutes* (PHOTO 4).

The napkins

For a 12-inch square napkin, cut a piece of fabric 14 inches square. Stitch a 1-inch hem around all four sides, then stencil them so that they match the tablecloth. Scale down the design and recut smaller stencils, or use the same ones that you used to print the tablecloth. Although the stencil design used to print the tablecloth may well be out of proportion to the size of the napkin, an interesting effect can be achieved by positioning these larger stencils so that parts of the design run off the edge of the napkin. If you like, you could also stitch each printed napkin to a larger piece of hemmed fabric to give it a border. Using the same material that you use to make the croissant tray will create a well-coordinated effect.

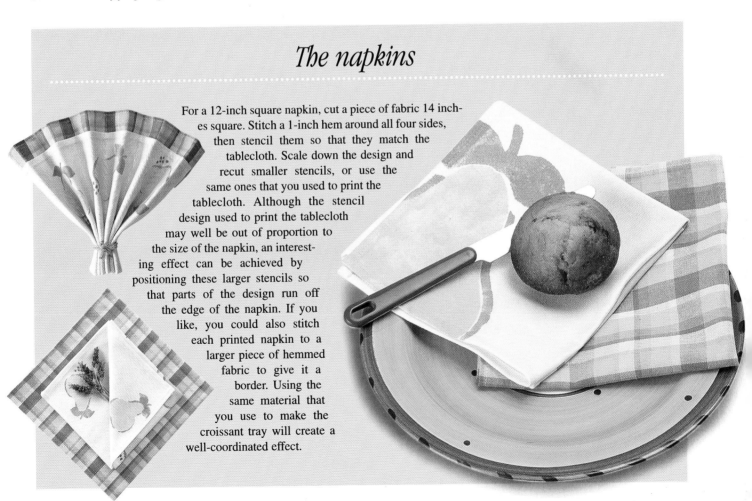

The croissant tray

Mix and match your fabrics and ribbons to make this attractive, reversible tray
for serving croissants, muffins or rolls at the table.

MATERIALS & EQUIPMENT

- ½ yard each of
two contrasting colors
of cotton fabric
- 1½ yards ribbon
about ⅜ inch wide;
color to match or contrast
with your fabric
- Sewing thread to match
the ribbons
- An 11½ x 17 inch sheet of
stiff cardboard
- Tape measure
- Scissors
- Ruler
- Dressmakers' pencil
- Pins
- Sewing machine

1. *Cut a square 15 inches x 15 inches from each fabric. Pin the two squares together with right sides facing.*

2. *Draw a stitching line 2¾ inch in from each edge of the material using a dressmakers' pencil (DIAGRAM 1).*

3. *Cut the ribbon into eight 6¼-inch lengths. Pin these between the two pieces of fabric at the stitching lines,*

⅝ inch from the edges of the fabric, securing ⅜ inch of each ribbon into the stitching line. The remaining 6 inches of ribbon must lie to the inside of the stitching line (DIAGRAM 2).

4. *Using the dotted lines in DIAGRAM 3 as a guide, stitch around the fabric, ⅜ inch in from the long edges and 7 cm 2¾ inches in at the corners, leaving one edge open.*

2¾ inches

2¾ inches

15 inches

DIAGRAM 1

DIAGRAM 2

DIAGRAM 3

5. *Trim away excess fabric close to the stitching line before turning right side out. Press the seams flat. The ribbons should now be anchored into the seams at the center of each short side.*

6. *Cut one piece of cardboard 9¼ inches square and four pieces each 2¼ inch x 9¼ inch. Insert a 2¼ inch x 9¼ inch piece of cardboard through the unstitched edge of the tray into each of the three side panels, and the square piece into the center. Draw a square around the central piece, joining the four inner corners. Carefully stitch along this line between the pieces of cardboard (DIAGRAM 4).*

7. *Insert the fourth 2¼ inch x 9¼ inch piece of cardboard into the unstitched side. Fold in a ⅜-inch seam allowance along the open edge and neatly hand-stitch closed.*

8. *Tie the ribbons into bows to bring together the sides of the tray. As the tray is completely reversible, this can be done with either fabric on the inside.*

DIAGRAM 4

Wrapped in ribbons

Ring the changes by adding extra ribbons and bows to the basic pattern for the croissant tray.

M A T E R I A L S & E Q U I P M E N T

You will need the same materials and equipment as for the tray on page 14, except that you will require 2½ yards of ⅜-inch ribbon in each of two different colors matching or contrasting with your fabric instead of 1½ yards.

1. *Cut each length of ribbon into four 22-inch lengths. Cut out the two pieces of fabric for the tray, each 15 inches square, then mark out a 2¼-inch square on each corner (DIAGRAM 1) and cut away these squares.*

2. *On the right side of one piece of fabric, pin a length of ribbon 1½ inches in from each long edge, and stitch these ribbons in place to within ⅜ inch of the short edges of the fabric (DIAGRAM 2). Repeat with the other square of fabric and the remaining ribbons, but sew them ⅝ inch in from the edge of the fabric.*

3. *Pin the two pieces of fabric to each other with right sides together, taking care to keep the ends of the ribbon lengths folded in towards the center so that they do not get stitched into the seam. Machine-stitch the pieces of fabric together right around the tray with a ⅜-inch seam, but leaving one end open.*

4. *Proceed as for STEPS 6-8 of the croissant tray, opposite.*

DIAGRAM 1

2 inches

2 inches

15 inches

DIAGRAM 2

The floral arrangement

You don't have to be a professional florist to produce a pleasing floral arrangement. Grouping flowers, herbs and fruit informally in an assortment of containers can achieve just the look that is needed to complement your bright breakfast table.

FRUIT WITH FLOWERS

Create a bold display with wild flowers and fruit still on the branch in a clutter of mismatched mugs and jugs. Small fruits such as berries and kumquats are ideal for this kind of arrangement, but larger, colorful fruits such as oranges or lemons with their leaves on can be equally decorative — simply pile them onto a plate or arrange in a bowl.

THE SINGLE COLOR DISPLAY

Colors that harmonize are easy to combine, yet they can produce a very effective display. Choose an assortment of flowers in shades of one color and arrange them separately in a variety of tall and short colored drinking glasses before grouping these together on the table.

SINGLE BLOOMS

Let individual flowers with distinctive shapes speak for themselves by placing single stems into separate containers such as simple glass bottles and grouping the containers together. Use both the height of the containers and the length of the flower stems to give the arrangement form. If a large arrangement in the middle of your table is going to take up too much space, place a single small flower in a small container at each place setting.

FLOATING FLOWERS

Snip the heads off full blooms and float them in water in an assortment of glass bowls and dishes. To make a strong statement, use a single, large bloom in a bowl of a similar size, or float smaller flower heads together to create a massed effect. Extra color can be introduced by tinting the water with food coloring, or by placing colored glass marbles or chips in the water, and you can also add a subtle fragrance to the air by adding flavorings such as orange essence.

CHAPTER TWO

Down to earth

If you can't have lunch in the country, bring a touch of the countryside
to your home with a combination of hand-painted enamelware,
a checked tablecloth and a bunch of wild flowers. The aroma of
sweet-smelling herbs encased in muslin bags will help to create just the
right atmosphere for a casual meal with friends.

The enamelware

You can paint a design on enamelware as easily as you would on paper. Simple geometric designs are probably easiest to work with, but use your imagination or draw inspiration from an endless number of sources such as books, magazines and fabrics for the designs of your choice. You may find some enamelware in secondhand shops, or you could try camping stores for new, inexpensive enamelware.

MATERIALS & EQUIPMENT

◆ Enamel plates, mugs and a jug
◆ Craft paint suitable for metal eating surfaces, in the colors of your choice
◆ Paper and a sharp pencil
◆ Ruler, protractor, pair of compasses, masking tape, tracing paper, carbon paper and self-adhesive dots (depending on your design all may be optional)
◆ Medium and fine paintbrushes

THE PLATES

As it is easier to work on a flat surface than a curved one, start by working on the plates, then move on to the mugs and jugs when you are comfortable with the technique.

1. *Work out your design on paper first, using one of the plates as a template to draw the circle so that you can plan your design to the exact size.*

2. *If you wish to follow the design shown here, it is important to work out the pattern repeat of the wavy border, or you may end up with an awkward section where the end of the line does not join up neatly with the starting point. The easiest way to do this is to divide the circle into equal segments before you start drawing. Find the diameter of the circle by folding the paper in quarters; the point where the two folds meet is the center of the circle. Place a protractor on the diameter line with its midpoint on the center, and*

DIAGRAM 1

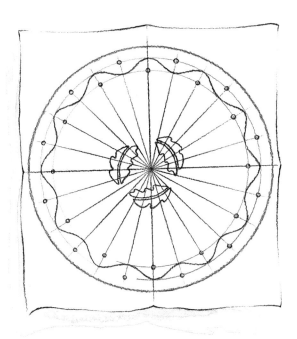

DIAGRAM 2

divide the 360° of the circle into equal slices (DIAGRAM 1). The size of these slices will determine the size of your pattern. Large slices will result in a very shallow wave, and small slices will give you a busier design. For an average dinner plate, 24 slices of 15° each will produce a pleasing pattern repeat.

3. Place the point of a pair of compasses in the center of the circle and draw two concentric circles, ³/16 inch and 1 inch in from the edge of the original circle. These will help you to draw waves of equal depth.

4. Carefully draw a continuous wavy line between these two circles, and draw dots on either side of the line to coincide with the 15° lines (DIAGRAM 2).

5. Draw the leaf pattern on PAGE 88 (TEMPLATE 2.1) in the center of the circle.

6. When you are satisfied with your rough design, you are ready to start painting the plate. Wipe the surface so that it is clean and free of dust. Transfer the leaf design onto the middle of the plate and the wavy line and dots onto the border with carbon paper (PHOTO 1). It may be easier to cut the center out of the paper design if your plate is deep. If you prefer, use a pencil to draw the design onto the plate. Any mistakes can be rubbed off with a soft cloth.

7. Paint the wavy line, then add the dots with the end of the paintbrush (PHOTO 2). Finally, paint in the leaves (PHOTO 3).

THE MUGS AND JUG

Follow the same technique applied to the plates to paint the mugs and jug. If you want your mugs to match your plates, paint the wavy border and dots around the top, then apply scaled-down leaves randomly over the rest of the surface. There is no need to worry about the border's pattern repeat, as the line will be interrupted by the handle. Note that when working out the design on your jug, remember to scale the pattern so that it is in proportion to the size of the jug.

Mix and match

If you stick to the same colors, there is no reason not to vary the designs on a mix-and-match set of mugs.

METHOD A

For a fun design, stick self-adhesive dots randomly over the surface of the mug. Make sure that they are well stuck down before applying paint in a ring around the dots; take care not to cover the dots, otherwise the paint may peel off as you lift them (PHOTO 1). When the paint is almost dry, carefully lift the edges of the stickers with the point of a craft knife and peel them off. Paint in the center of the dots in the same color or a contrasting color, leaving a small gap between each dot and the ring of color unpainted to edge the dots (PHOTO 2).

METHOD B

Use masking tape to mask off the top of the mug. Draw evenly spaced vertical lines in pencil and paint in alternate stripes in the color of your choice (PHOTO 3). This can be done freehand, or you can use masking tape for neater edges. Carefully remove the masking tape while the paint is still wet so that the paint does not peel off with the tape. When the stripes have dried, paint in the wavy border and dots as you did for the plates.

METHOD C

For a really simple alternative, paint the whole mug in bold, vertical stripes as described above, but leaving off the wavy border and dots.

1

2

3

All tied up

Replace the conventional napkin ring with a few simple alternatives using inexpensive, easy-to-obtain materials such as raffia, corrugated cardboard, cotton string and fresh herbs.

METHOD A *(right)*

1. *Cut nine lengths of raffia, each about 24 inches long. Tie these together with a knot about 1⅝ inch from one end. Divide the lengths into three lots of three and plait them to within 1⅝ inch of the other end. Tie a knot to secure the plait.* **2.** *Fold the napkin in half and roll it up lengthways. Wind the raffia plait around the roll three times and tie the ends into a knot.*

METHOD B *(above)*

1. *Cut a 2 inch x 6 inch rectangle of corrugated cardboard, its length running across the corrugations.* **2.** *Roll up the napkin as described above.* **3.** *Wrap the cardboard strip around the roll and tie a length of cotton string around it to hold it in place. Tie the ends into a neat bow.*

METHOD D *(below)*

1. *Cut a rectangular piece of brown paper about 2 inches x 6 inches.* **2.** *Roll up the napkin as described in* METHOD A *and wrap the paper strip around the roll. Hold this in place with a small piece of adhesive tape.* **3.** *Drip sealing wax onto the adhesive tape to conceal it, and use a seal, ring or coin to make a decorative impression before the wax sets.*

METHOD C *(above)*

1. *Cut a 1¾-inch section from the cardboard core of a toilet roll or paper towel roll.* **2.** *Stick the end of a length of raffia to the inside of the core with masking tape. Cover the entire core by winding raffia through the center and around the outside. As raffia comes in quite short lengths, you will probably have to join several pieces; don't try to conceal the knots, as they add to the overall effect.* **3.** *Stick the end of the raffia to the inside of the core with masking tape.*

METHOD E *(below)*

1. *Form a piece of florists' wire into a ring about 2¾ inches in diameter. Roll up the napkin and slide the wire ring over.* **2.** *Carefully wind cuttings of fresh herbs around the ring to conceal the wire and create a truly fresh herbal napkin ring. These rings must be prepared on the day they are to be used, as the herbs will wilt within hours of being cut.*

Herb sachets

Muslin bags filled with aromatic herbs make inexpensive gifts for lunch guests and add a decorative touch to a rustic table setting. To dry herbs, hang bunches of them upside down in a protected, dry place for a week or so, or leave them in a warm oven for a few hours. When dry, crumble them to release their scent.

MATERIALS & EQUIPMENT

◆ Muslin cloth – one 12-inch square per sachet for METHOD A or 12 inches x 4 inches per sachet for METHOD B
◆ 16 inches of jute string, raffia or ribbon for each sachet
◆ Assorted dried herbs
◆ Needle or sewing machine and cotton thread for METHOD B
◆ Safety pin or tapestry needle

METHOD A

1. *Cut a circular piece of muslin, using a plate with a diameter of 10 inches as a template to mark out the circle.*

2. *Place a small handful of dried herbs in the center of the circle.*

3. *Gather up the muslin around the herbs, and tie a length of ribbon, string or raffia into a knot around this. Tie the ends into a neat bow and fan the muslin out above this.*

METHOD B

1. *Fold the rectangle of muslin in half to form a 4 inch x 6 inch rectangle. Stitch a seam down each side to form a bag.*

2. *Turn the bag right side out, then fold down the top 1¼ inch of fabric towards the inside. Stitch down all the way round, 1 inch from the folded top edge.*

3. *Form a casing for a drawstring by sewing a second row of stitching* ⅜ inch up from your first stitching line. Carefully unpick the side seam of the bag between the two rows of stitching to insert the ribbon.

4. *Using a safety pin or a needle with a large eye, thread a 12-inch length of ribbon, string or raffia through the casing, leaving enough of a "tail" on the outside to tie in a bow once the bag is drawn closed (PHOTO 1).*

5. *Fill the bag with dried herbs, pull the drawstrings and tie into a neat bow.*

The tablemats

In this reverse appliqué technique the leaf design is cut out of a piece of fabric to reveal a different fabric beneath. The richly contrasting colors used here were chosen to coordinate with the painted enamelware, but if you prefer more muted shades, try finding fabrics with contrasting textures or patterns instead.

M A T E R I A L S & E Q U I P M E N T

FOR EACH TABLEMAT YOU WILL NEED:

◆ Two 17 inch x 13 inch pieces of red fabric

◆ One 17 inch x 13 inch piece of green cotton fabric

◆ Sewing thread to match the red fabric

◆ Dressmakers' carbon paper and tracing wheel

◆ Pins and a needle

◆ A sharp pair of scissors

3. *Turn the cut edge of the leaf outline under by ⅜ inch (along the dotted line), snipping the fabric where necessary, and hand-stitch the top piece of fabric to the bottom one with neat running stitches just inside the turned edge (PHOTO 2).*

4. *Lay the second piece of red fabric on top of the first piece (which is now attached to the green piece in the middle by the appliqué stitches). Pin all three layers together and stitch a ⅜-inch seam around three and a half sides, leaving an opening large enough for the mat to be turned the right way out.*

5. *Trim the seam and turn the mat right side out through the unstitched opening (PHOTO 3). Press the seams flat and hand-stitch the opening closed.*

1. *Enlarge the leaf design on* PAGE 88 (TEMPLATE 2.2) *on a photocopier so that the leaf measures about 10 inches x 13 inches. Transfer the design onto the center of one piece of red fabric with a tracing wheel and dressmakers' carbon* (PHOTO 1).

2. *Cut out the leaf shape along the solid line. Pin the piece of red fabric to the green fabric and tack it down about 1 inch from the edge of the design.*

CHAPTER THREE

Tea for two

Teatime is a special time of indulgence, so take out your best china and lay it out on a table decked with the prettiest appliquéd tablemats and napkins, muffin holder and jam jar. Strawberries and cream set the theme for the appliqué motifs and the hand-painted jam jar.

The tablemats

These floral tablemats are framed by a border of green checked fabric and decorated with an appliquéd strawberry in one corner. If you prefer a simpler look, use a checked fabric (such as gingham) in the center and matching plain fabric for the border.

MATERIALS & EQUIPMENT

FOR EACH TABLEMAT YOU WILL NEED:

- A 12 inch x 18 inch piece of floral cotton fabric
- A 16 inch x 22 inch piece of green checked fabric to match the floral fabric
- Small pieces of red and green cotton fabric for the appliqué design
- A 12 inch x 18 inch piece of thin polyester batting for quilting
- Iron-on interfacing
- Sewing thread to match your fabric
- White and black thread for the appliqué design
- Water-soluble fabric marker pen
- Ruler
- Sewing machine
- Sharp scissors
- Paper, tracing paper and pencil
- Needle and pins

1. *Lay the 16 inch x 22 inch piece of checked fabric on a flat surface. Use a water-soluble fabric marker pen and a ruler to mark a 12 inch x 18 inch rectangle in the centre of the piece of fabric, leaving a 2-inch border all round* (DIAGRAM 1).

2. *Lay the rectangle of batting onto this marked rectangle, and then the floral rectangle on top of this. Tack the layers together to hold them in place. Use the water-soluble pen and ruler to mark light diagonal lines, 2 inches apart, across the fabric. Machine-stitch along these lines through all three layers* (DIAGRAM 2).

3. *Fold in each corner of the unquilted border of checked fabric diagonally, so that the middle of the diagonal fold meets the corner of the quilted section* (DIAGRAM 3). *Press the fold flat with an iron, then cut off the corner of the larger rectangle of fabric ¼ inch in from the fold.*

4. *Fold in the flaps of the larger piece of material and stitch the diagonal seams neatly by hand* (DIAGRAM 4). *Tack the folded border in place, and finish by stitching the raw edge with a fine zigzag stitch through all thicknesses. If you wish, stitch a second row of zigzag stitches on the border ⅝ inch from the first row.*

5. *To make the strawberries for the corner, trace the two components of the fruit design given on* PAGE 88 (TEMPLATES 3.1 AND 3.2) *and transfer onto paper. Carefully cut out these shapes to use as templates.*

6. *Cut a square of red fabric for the strawberry and green for the leaves, and press iron-on interfacing onto the back of each piece of fabric to stiffen it and make it easier to work with. Place the templates on the pieces of fabric and pin them in position. Carefully cut around the templates.*

16 inches

12 inches

18 inches

22 inches

DIAGRAM 1

DIAGRAM 2

7. *Place the strawberry cutout on a piece of backing fabric a little larger than the berry and leaves, and tack it in position. Set your sewing machine to a fine zigzag stitch and thread it with white thread. Carefully stitch around the shape, sewing into every point and curve. Make sure that the entire edge of the motif is sewn, otherwise the fabric will soon fray around the stitching* (PHOTO 1).

8. *Position the cut-out leaf and stalk on top of the berry shape. Tack it in place and zigzag around the shape. Hand-stitch small, black dots on the strawberry and sew into the leaf shape with white thread, following the dotted lines on the leaf template on* PAGE 88 (TEMPLATE 3.2).

9. *Carefully cut out the finished strawberry motif. Attach it neatly to one corner of the tablemat by stitching by hand from the underside of the mat so that the stitches are not seen on the surface* (PHOTO 2). *Make enough strawberries for one corner of each mat or, if you prefer, decorate all four corners on each mat.*

DIAGRAM 3

DIAGRAM 4

The napkins

These napkins coordinate with the tablemats to continue the strawberry theme, using a simplified version of the appliqué technique to decorate them.

MATERIALS & EQUIPMENT

FOR EACH NAPKIN YOU WILL NEED:

- A 12 inch x 12 inch square of green checked fabric to match the tablemats
- 1½ yards narrow bias binding in a color to match your fabric
- Sewing thread to match your fabric

- White and black thread
- Small pieces of red and green cotton fabric for the appliqué design
- Iron-on interfacing
- Sharp scissors
- Pins and needle
- Sewing machine
- Paper, tracing paper and pencil

1. *Round off the corners of the square of fabric. Open out one side of the bias binding and pin it all the way round the square, starting in the middle of one side. Stitch the binding down its fold line, easing it carefully around the corners.*

2. *Fold the binding over the raw edge of the fabric. Neatly slip-stitch it to the other side, overlapping the starting point by ⅜ inch and tucking in the raw ends* (PHOTO 1).

3. *Photocopy the two components of the strawberry motif on PAGE 88, reducing their size if you wish. Cut out the shapes. Cut a square of red fabric for the berry and green fabric for the leaves. Press iron-on interfacing on the back to stiffen the fabric. Pin the templates to the pieces of fabric and carefully cut out the motifs.*

4. *Position the berry shape in one corner of the napkin, tack in place, then stitch down directly onto the napkin with a fine zigzag stitch (as in STEP 7 of the tablemat instructions). Finish by appliquéing the leaves* (PHOTO 2), *as described in STEP 8 of the tablemat instructions.*

The jam jar

You can buy cold ceramic paints that are specially formulated for applying to glazed ceramics. These dry within a few hours and do not require firing in a kiln. Although they are for decorative rather than utilitarian use, making them unsuitable for plates, they are fine for painting a jam jar to match your table setting.

MATERIALS & EQUIPMENT

◆ A plain white, glazed ceramic jam jar – buy an inexpensive one from a shop that sells kitchenware
◆ Green, red and black ceramic paints (available at craft shops)
◆ Pencil
◆ Tracing paper
◆ Carbon paper
◆ Masking tape
◆ A fine paintbrush for painting the design, and a cocktail stick for painting in the dots

1. *Trace the whole strawberry design given on* PAGE 88 (TEMPLATE 3.3) *onto a small piece of tracing paper.*

2. *Cut a piece of carbon paper the same size as the tracing paper and place it on the jam jar, carbon side down. Lay the tracing paper on the carbon paper and*

hold it in place with small pieces of masking tape. Draw over the design with a pencil to transfer it onto the jar (PHOTO 1). *Repeat the motif over the whole jar and lid. If you are not happy with any part of the design, simply wipe off the traced lines and redo the motif.*

3. *Starting with red, paint in the berries* (PHOTO 2). *When these are dry, paint in the green stalks and leaves and again leave to dry.*

4. *Finally, apply small dots to the strawberries with a cocktail stick and black paint* (PHOTO 3).

5. *When the paint is dry, bake according to the manufacturer's instructions.*

The muffin holder

Match the fabric of the tablemats and napkins for this muffin or scone holder, which has eight pockets. Alternatively, you may want to mix and match your own choice of fabrics; as long as you select fabrics with harmonious colors, you can be assured of a successful end result.

M A T E R I A L S & E Q U I P M E N T

◆ 12 inches x 36 inches each of floral and green checked cotton fabric to match the tablemats and napkins

◆ A 12 inch x 12 inch polyester piece of batting

◆ 2¾ yards narrow bias binding in a color to match your fabrics

◆ Sewing thread to match your fabrics

◆ Press studs

◆ 12 inches of ribbon, ⅜-inch wide

◆ Round bread basket, 10 inches in diameter

◆ Paper and pencil

◆ Scissors

◆ Pins and needle

◆ Sewing machine

◆ Water-soluble fabric marker pen

◆ A ruler

DIAGRAM 1

DIAGRAM 2

DIAGRAM 4

1. *Using a dinner plate as a guide, draw a circle 10 inches in diameter on paper. Cut this out and use it as a pattern to cut two circles from each piece of fabric.*

2. *Take one circle of each fabric and pin them to each other with wrong sides together. Repeat with the other pair of circles. Bind each pair of circles with the bias binding. The neatest way of doing this is to open out one side of the binding and pin it around the edge of the circle, stitch it in place along the fold line of the binding (*DIAGRAM 1*), fold the binding over the raw edges of the fabric and neatly slip-stitch it in place (*DIAGRAM 2*).*

3. *Place one bound circle on top of the other with the checked fabric uppermost on both. Stitch these two circles together with two lines of stitching running*

through the centre of the circle at right angles to one another (DIAGRAM 3).

4. *Stitch the press-stud halves to the edge of the top circle as shown in* DIAGRAM 4. *Cut two 6-inch lengths of ribbon and hand-stitch each piece to the edge of the top circle next to the press studs.*

5. *Cut a 11-inch square from each of the fabrics and from the batting. Sandwich the batting between the fabric squares, so that the right sides of the squares of fabric are facing outwards, and then tack the layers together to hold them in place.*

6. *Using a water-soluble fabric pen and a ruler, lightly mark quilting lines, 2 inches apart, in a criss-cross pattern on the fabric. Machine-stitch along the lines through all three layers of fabric.*

7. *Use your paper pattern to cut a circle from the quilted fabric. Neaten the edge with an overlock stitch and bind it with the bias binding, as described in* STEP 2.

8. *Lay the quilted circle on your working surface with the floral fabric uppermost. Lay the joined circles, with the checked fabric uppermost, on top of the quilted one. Pin the lower unquilted fabric circle to the quilted one, then carefully stitch these two together in the form of a cross, with the lines of stitching running between those that join the top two circles and as far in to the center as you can go. Snap the press studs on the edges of the top circle together so that the fabric doesn't get in the way while you sew (*DIAGRAM 5*).*

9. *Neatly tie the ribbons into a bow and place the finished holder in the basket.*

DIAGRAM 3

DIAGRAM 5

CHAPTER FOUR

Simply fishy

Get in tune with nature and set the scene for an outdoor meal, using
simple decorating techniques and some basic materials to deck out your table.
Create the mood of the seaside with a fish motif and carry the
theme through with pebbles and shells.

The tablemats and napkins

There are numerous ways of repeating a motif or pattern. For example, you can make a stencil,
as described in chapter 1, use carbon paper to transfer the design, then paint it in, as described in chapter 2, or buy
a rubber stamp from a craft shop. Here, an alternative technique, which is both simple and cost-effective,
successfully combines a sponged-on motif with stenciling.

MATERIALS & EQUIPMENT

- ◆ A 11½ inch x 17 inch sheet of white paper for each tablemat
- ◆ Good quality white paper napkins
- ◆ Beige and blue acrylic paint
- ◆ Clear acetate film
- ◆ Sharp craft knife

- ◆ Fine-tipped permanent marker
- ◆ Pencil and ruler
- ◆ Masking tape
- ◆ Sponge
- ◆ Paper towel or newspaper

2.5 cm (1 in)

2.5 cm (1 in)

1 inch

DIAGRAM 1

1. Start by making a stencil for the rope border. Cut a piece of acetate film 15 inches x 4 inches in size. Place this over the rope template on PAGE 89 and use a permanent marker to trace the design until you have drawn 13 inches of "rope." Carefully cut out the design with a sharp craft knife.

2. Using a pencil and ruler, lightly draw a rectangle on the sheet of 11½ x 17 inch paper. This will serve as a guide for positioning the edges of the stencil. Make a mark 1 inch along the drawn lines from each corner of the rectangle to indicate where the strips of stenciled rope design should start and finish.

3. Position the stencil on the inside of the guide line and hold it in place with masking tape (DIAGRAM 1). To remove excess stickiness and prevent the tape from tearing the paper when the stencil is lifted, stick the tape onto a piece of fabric before applying it.

4. Pour a small quantity of beige paint into a saucer. Dip a small piece of sponge into the paint and dab off any excess on a paper towel or newspaper. Very little paint is required and the sponge should be as dry as possible to prevent bleeding under the edges of the stencil. Apply the paint to the cut-out area of the stencil with a daubing motion (PHOTO 1).

5. Carefully remove the stencil and reposition it on one of the other sides. Stencil all four sides, masking off some of the cut stencil for the shorter sides. Set the paper aside while you prepare the fish and starfish motifs.

6. Draw fish and starfish designs (TEMPLATES 4.2 AND 4.3 ON PAGE 89) onto a sponge with a felt-tipped pen. Cut out the designs with a craft knife (PHOTO 2).

7. Starting with the starfish motif, dip the sponge into the same paint that you used for the rope border. Again, daub off any excess and position the sponge in the corner of the border (see photo on PAGE 36). Press it lightly onto the paper, and repeat in the other three corners.

8. Fill in the center of the tablemat with fish applied in the same way as the starfish, but using the blue paint (PHOTO 3). You could plan the positioning of each motif, but this is time-consuming and not really necessary, as a random scattering of fish produces a casual and far more pleasing result.

9. If you have access to a plastic laminating service (offered by speciality outlets), you may want to laminate your tablemats to preserve them. If not, the amount of time and money spent on the mats is minimal, so you can afford to throw them away after the meal and make more when you need them again.

10. Use either the shell sponge or the fish sponge to decorate one corner of each paper napkin (PHOTO 4).

The tray

A sponge technique similar to that used for the tablemats and napkins is used here to decorate a wooden tray. In this case, however, the fish motif is created by sponging on a number of small squares to give the design the appearance of an intricate mosaic.

MATERIALS & EQUIPMENT

◆ A rectangular
wooden tray. If you can't
find a plain one, you will need
to get rid of as much of the
paint or varnish as possible
with paint stripper
or sandpaper
◆ Wood primer
◆ White undercoat
◆ Light gray, black,
white, blue and beige
acrylic paints
◆ Clear varnish
◆ Paintbrushes
◆ Carbon paper
◆ Pencil
◆ Synthetic sponge
◆ Ruler
◆ Felt-tipped pen
◆ Sharp craft knife
◆ Paper towel or newspaper
◆ Soft, lint-free cloth

1. *Apply a coat of wood primer to the tray with a paintbrush and allow it to dry thoroughly.*

2. *Give the tray two good coats of white undercoat, allowing the paint to dry between coats. Then apply a coat of light gray paint to the upper surface of the base of the tray and allow to dry thoroughly* (PHOTO 1).

3. *Using a photocopier, enlarge the fish design* (TEMPLATE 4.4) *given on* PAGE 89 *until it fits comfortably into the base of your tray. There should be a gap of about 2-2½ inches between the edges of the tray and the head and tail of the fish to allow space for the painted border and the background.*

4. *Lay a sheet of carbon paper, carbon-side down, on the tray and position the fish design on top. Draw over the design with a pencil to transfer it onto the tray.*

5. *Use a felt-tipped pen and ruler to mark out a few ½-inch squares on the sponge, then cut these out with a sharp craft knife* (PHOTO 2). *These blocks will be used to apply paint in a way that will create a mosaic effect.*

6. *Place a small quantity of each of the black, blue, beige and white paint colors on a mixing tray. Dip a sponge block into the black paint, daub off any excess paint on a piece of paper towel or newspaper, and press the sponge onto the tray in a corner. Repeat in a line around all four sides, leaving small gaps in between each square as you would if you were working an actual mosaic* (PHOTO 3). *Work*

two rows in black, then fill in the rest of the area surrounding the fish design with squares of beige paint.

7. Outline the fish's body with a row of black squares, then fill in the body, tail and fins with blue and beige (PHOTO 4). Create a range of blues and beiges by

blending in touches of white to lighten them and black for darker shades. Try to avoid overlapping squares, although the fish shape will make this unavoidable in places. For really tricky bits, you could cut the sponge into smaller shapes. Make the fish's eye black and sponge in the surrounding area in white.

8. When the paint is completely dry, mix some white paint with about five times as much water. Rub this over the tray with a soft cloth to soften the lines and give the surface an aged look (PHOTO 5).

9. Seal the tray with two or three coats of varnish, allowing it to dry between coats.

Shell details

You will need an assortment of shells for these projects. If you live near the sea, it is easy to collect them. Otherwise ask a friend who does to send you some, or buy shells from a specialty store or gift shop.

THE TABLECLOTH

To weight your tablecloth down and prevent it from blowing away, sew individual shells along the edge of the cloth and clusters at the corners. Choose shells that are similar in shape or go for a mix-and-match look; just make sure that they are about the same size. Drill small holes through them, using a hand drill with a small masonry bit, then sew them at regular intervals along the edge of the cloth with a strong thread. For the corners, choose larger shells and group them together.

THE NAPKIN TIES

Match the shell detail and stenciled rope border with some simple napkin ties to dress up your printed paper napkins. Cut a 14-inch length of thin cotton rope. Tie a knot at either end, and sew a shell to each knot as you did along the hem of the tablecloth. Roll up your napkin or shape it into a loose cone by pinching it up at its center point and shaking out the folds of the napkin, then tie the length of shell-decorated rope around it.

THE CANDLES

Floating candles are ideal for outdoors — simply float them below the rim of a bowl to protect the flame from the wind.

Melt plain white candles in an old double boiler or a large can over simmering water, until the wax liquifies. If you want to make colored candles, add wax colorant or pieces of wax crayon to the melting candles. Remove the wicks and set aside to re-use in the new candles. Pour the melted wax into plastic or metal shell-shaped molds (available from cooks' specialty stores), or use half shells if available. Tie a small weight to one end of each wick, then insert a wick in the center of each mold and suspend it until the wax sets. Trim the wicks, leaving about ½ inch protruding from the top of each candle.

Ease the candles out of the molds, or if you are using shells, let them remain in the shells. Place some washed pebbles and shells at the bottom of a glass bowl. Fill the bowl about three-quarters full with water, and float the candles in it. If you wish, add a little food coloring to the water.

Frosted glassware

Creating the effect of etching on glass does not take any special talent or expensive equipment. Simply stencil your design on with vinyl contact plastic and glass etching fluid, available from hardware stores or craft shops.

MATERIALS & EQUIPMENT

◆ Glasses
◆ Glass etching fluid
◆ Tracing paper and pencil
◆ Vinyl contact plastic
◆ A sharp craft knife
◆ A small paintbrush

1. *Photocopy the fish and/or starfish designs on* PAGE 89 *(*TEMPLATES 4.2 AND 4.3*), reducing their size if you wish, and transfer the design(s) onto small pieces of contact plastic.*

2. *Cut out the shapes with a craft knife, position the contact plastic on the outside of a glass, then stick it in place (*PHOTO 1*). Rub the plastic down well to ensure that the etching fluid does not bleed under the edges of the stencil.*

3. *Paint a layer of etching fluid onto the exposed area (*PHOTO 2*). Leave it to dry for a few minutes before removing the contact paper and washing the glass.*

NOTE: If you cut out the stencil shapes carefully, you could also use the positive shape of the same design to etch some of the glasses.

CHAPTER FIVE

Art on the table

A bright assortment of decorative products created predominantly from paper is combined with a collection of cheerful china and boldly colored cutlery to set the mood for an informal dinner party. Try your hand at a papier-mâché bowl and napkin holders, decoupage tablemats and a bunch of paper poppies.

The bowl and napkin holders

Papier-mâché is not just for children. Constructed carefully and imaginatively decorated, these table accessories will make an interesting and original feature on your table. Make a bold statement with simple geometric patterns and bright colors, or use the decoupage mats for inspiration.

MATERIALS & EQUIPMENT

- ◆ Newspaper
- ◆ Petroleum jelly
- ◆ Wallpaper paste
- ◆ Thin cardboard
- ◆ Masking tape
- ◆ White acrylic paint
- ◆ Gouache paints in the colors of your choice
- ◆ Non-toxic clear varnish
- ◆ Scissors
- ◆ Sharp craft knife
- ◆ Pencil
- ◆ Thick and thin paintbrushes

FOR THE BOWL YOU WILL ALSO NEED:
- ◆ A mold, such as a plastic or glass bowl, or a flat-topped metal lampshade; your choice will determine the shape of the finished product.

FOR THE NAPKIN HOLDERS YOU WILL ALSO NEED:
- ◆ Embroidery thread
- ◆ A piece of stiff card
- ◆ A sewing needle
- ◆ Two beads for each napkin holder

4. Make a base for the bowl by cutting a circle of cardboard the same diameter as the bottom of the bowl and securing it to the outside with masking tape (PHOTO 3).

5. Apply two more layers of pasted strips to cover both the inside and the outside of the bowl, and leave to dry completely.

6. Paint the bowl with two coats of white paint to give it a smooth surface.

7. When the paint has dried, pencil your design lightly onto the painted surface. Fill in the design with gouache paints, starting with the lightest color and working through to the darkest (PHOTO 4).

8. When thoroughly dry, seal the bowl with two layers of clear varnish.

THE BOWL

1. Tear the newspaper into strips 4-6 inches long and ¾-1⅛ inches wide. Spread a thin layer of petroleum jelly over the outside of the mold.

2. Mix the wallpaper paste according to the instructions on the packet. Soak strips of paper in the paste and apply them to the mold, one layer at a time, extending them beyond the rim by about 1 inch (PHOTO 1). Apply eight to

ten layers, leaving each layer to dry before applying the next.

3. When the final layer of paper has dried completely, trim the top and bottom edges of the bowl with scissors (PHOTO 2). Insert a knife carefully between the mold and the papier-mâché shell to loosen and separate the two. Remove the hardened bowl from the mold and bind the top edge carefully with small strips of pasted paper to neaten it.

THE NAPKIN HOLDERS

1. *Roll a 6½-inch square of cardboard into a cone. Secure the join with masking tape. Cut the open-end level so that the card is the size and shape of a large ice-cream cone (DIAGRAM 1).*

2. *Proceed as for the bowl, pasting small strips of paper onto the outside and over the top edge to the inside. Work carefully for the first couple of layers as you do not have a solid base to work on.*

3. *Paint the cone, following STEPS 6-8 of the bowl (opposite).*

4. *To make the tassels, wrap embroidery thread around a piece of stiff cardboard cut as wide as the desired length of the tassels, until there is enough for the fullness you require. Secure the threads with a knot (DIAGRAM 2). Slide them off the card and wrap more thread around them tightly, just below the top (DIAGRAM 3). Cut the loops of thread at the bottom.*

5. *Finally attach the tassel to the cone. Thread a needle with embroidery thread and knot the ends. Insert the needle through the top of the tassel, then through the eye of a bead and into the point of the cone. Bring the needle through a second bead on the inside of the cone, back through to the outside of the cone and again through the eye of the first bead (DIAGRAM 4). Pull the thread tight and secure it in the tassel, then trim the ends.*

DIAGRAM 3

DIAGRAM 1

DIAGRAM 2

DIAGRAM 4

The tablemats

Decoupage is the application of decorative paper cutouts to a surface. Flat tablemats are ideally suited to this craft, and the design possibilities are endless, but if you want mats that are a nonstandard shape they may have to be specially cut. You can also use the technique to give old cork-backed mats a facelift. For the cutouts, choose suitable floral wrapping paper. The designs should have clearly defined outlines that will be easy to cut around.

1. *Paint the plywood with wood primer. When dry, apply two coats of acrylic paint, allowing drying time between coats.*

2. *Cut out the flowers from the patterned paper with scissors or a craft knife. Lay the cutouts on the dry, painted surface of the mat. When you are happy with the arrangement, stick the paper cutouts down with glue, ensuring that each piece is firmly attached* (PHOTO 1).

3. *When dry, apply two to three coats of clear varnish to seal and protect the mat.*

4. *Stick felt to the back of the mat with glue* (PHOTO 2), *and when dry, carefully trim the edges of the felt.*

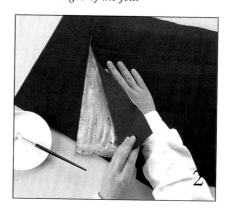

MATERIALS & EQUIPMENT

FOR EACH MAT YOU WILL NEED:

◆ A 12 inch x 16 inch piece of thin plywood or masonite
◆ Wood primer
◆ Acrylic paint in the color of your choice
◆ Assorted pictures of flowers
◆ Clear varnish
◆ PVA glue
◆ Felt for backing
◆ Sharp craft scissors or craft knife
◆ Paintbrushes

Paper poppies

These cheerful paper poppies are so easy to make, and provide a colorful way to liven up any table setting.

MATERIALS & EQUIPMENT

- ◆ Red crepe paper
- ◆ Black crepe paper
- ◆ Thick florist's wire
- ◆ Cotton wool
- ◆ Green florist's tape
- ◆ Thin florists' binding wire
- ◆ Sharp scissors or a craft knife
- ◆ Black pencil crayon

1. *Enlarge the petal pattern* (TEMPLATE 5.1 ON PAGE 90) *on a photocopier by 141% and transfer the shape onto the red crepe paper with the arrow on the diagram pointing in the direction of the*

grain of the paper. Cut out six petals with scissors or a craft knife; if you layer the crepe paper you will be able to cut out all six petals at once.

2. *If you wish, use a black pencil crayon to draw detail lines on each petal. Cup the petals by holding the center of each*

between your thumbs and forefingers and gently pushing and stretching the paper outwards to the sides (PHOTO 1).

3. *Cut a 1 inch x 8 inch strip of black crepe paper across the grain. Enlarge* TEMPLATE 5.2 *on* PAGE 90 *by 141% and use it to cut a ⅜-inch fringe along one long edge.*

4. *Insert the end of a piece of thick florist's wire into the center of a small ball of cotton wool. Cut a black crepe paper circle 2¼ inches in diameter, wrap it around the cotton wool, and fasten it to the florist's wire (the stem) with tape* (PHOTO 2).

5. *Gather the black paper fringe in your fingers, wrap it around the covered center, and secure it by wrapping thin binding wire around the stem* (PHOTO 3).

6. *Take the petals one at a time and gather the bottom edges, then cluster them around the poppy center, over-lapping them and securing them with thin florist's binding wire* (PHOTO 4).

7. *Working from the top of the stem, use green florist's tape to cover the base of the poppy center and petals, and to wrap the entire stem* (PHOTO 5).

CHAPTER SIX

Putting on the glitz

Guests will be convinced that no expense has been spared in creating this lavish setting. But the clever use of fabric and a touch of gold proves that all that glitters need not cost a fortune.

The swagged tablecloth

A long undercloth in a subtle cream check is covered by a plain cream cloth, gathered up at intervals around the sides of the table to reveal the contrasting fabric. The edges of the top cloth are decorated with charming bunches of ivy and gold or cream bows at the gathers, providing a colorful accent and a counterpoint to the fruity centerpiece.

MATERIALS & EQUIPMENT

- Two tablecloths in coordinating fabrics; the bottom cloth should be as long as possible, preferably down to the ground, and the top cloth must have a drop of at least 24 inches
- Narrow curtain tape
- Cream sewing thread
- Gold or cream ribbon
- Sprigs of ivy and, if you wish, flowers and berries
- Thin florist's binding wire
- Gold spray paint
- Tape measure
- Ruler
- Water-soluble fabric marker pen
- Extra-long pins

DIAGRAM 1

4. *Lay the bottom cloth on the table and top it with the swagged cloth. Tie bunches of ivy with the florist's wire (*PHOTO *3). You can also include flowers or sprays of berries, but you will have to prepare these very close to the time when you need them, as the flowers will soon wilt if kept out of water. Lightly spray the ivy with gold paint so that the leaves are just touched with gold (*PHOTO *4).*

5. *Wrap a length of ribbon around the ivy to cover the wire, and tie it into a generous bow. Use long pins to attach the bunches to the cloth between the swags at the edge of the table (*PHOTO *5).*

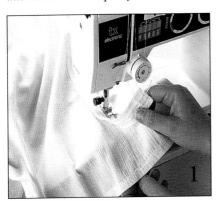

1. *Lay the top tablecloth upside down on your table, ensuring that the drop is even all the way around. If the table is square or rectangular, measure the sides and divide this measurement into equal parts of between 20 inches and 40 inches each. Use a water-soluble fabric marker to mark these points at the edge of the table and the points where the cloth will drape over the corners of the table. If your cloth is round or oval, measure its circumference and divide this measurement equally.*

2. *Remove the cloth from the table and lay it out flat, again upside down. Draw lines from the marks to the edge of the cloth as shown in* DIAGRAM *1.*

3. *Stitch lengths of narrow curtain tape along these lines (*PHOTO *1). Tie a knot in the drawstrings at one end of the tape. Pulling the other end of the drawstrings, gather up each section tightly (*PHOTO *2). Tie the long end of the drawstrings into a bow so that they can be undone when the cloth is washed.*

The chairs

These chair covers are very simple to assemble. They consist of two rectangles of fabric — preferably the same fabric as you used for the undercloth on the table — draped across each other over the chair and tied together with ribbons to hold them in place.

MATERIALS & EQUIPMENT

FOR EACH CHAIR YOU WILL NEED:
◆ A length of cream fabric
to match your tablecloth
(see Measuring the fabric, page 53)
◆ 4 yards gold or cream ribbon
◆ Water-soluble fabric marker pen
◆ Cream sewing thread
◆ Tape measure
◆ Pins

The candle shades

These shaded candles will cast a warm light over your table without the glare of an open flame. Candle carriers — the metal supports for the shades — fit neatly over the top of the candles.

MATERIALS & EQUIPMENT

- Candle carriers (available from decorating outlets)
- Brown paper or newsprint
- Handmade paper – a 17 inch x 23 inch sheet will make one shade
- Adhesive and double-sided tape
- Gold ribbon
- Brass split fasteners
- Ruler
- Pair of compasses
- Scissors
- Punch

1. *First make a template for the shade from brown paper or newsprint. Measure the diameter of the top of the candle carrier, then draw two concentric circles with the compasses — the first an inch larger than the diameter of the carrier and the second about four times the diameter of the first. Draw a straight line from* the center of the circle to any point on the circumference of the larger circle. Cut along this line, then cut along the circumference of each drawn circle (DIAGRAM 1).

2. *Wrap the template around the candle carrier so that the ends overlap, and hold them in place with a small piece of adhesive tape* (PHOTO 1). *Mark the overlap, then remove the tape and flatten the paper. Trim the overlap to within 1 inch of the marked line.*

3. *Lay the template on the handmade paper, trace around it, then carefully cut out the shape.*

4. *Punch holes at intervals of about ¾ inch near the bottom edge of the shade.*

5. *Stick the shade together with double-sided tape. Insert brass paper fasteners down the seam* (PHOTO 2), *thread narrow gold ribbon through the holes, binding the edge of the paper* (PHOTO 3), *and tie the ends in a bow.*

6. *Put your candle into a candlestick, press the carrier down onto the candle, then place the shade on top.*

2

DIAGRAM 1

1

3

CHAPTER SEVEN

Party plan

It's a special occasion, so why not celebrate in style?
Choose a party theme with an elegant black and white color scheme,
and carry it through from the invitations to the namecards
and menus, candle holders and gift boxes.

The invitations

Many stationery shops stock blank invitation cards, but creating your own personalized cards will set the tone for your party and give guests a hint of the theme you have chosen for the special night.

MATERIALS & EQUIPMENT

FOR EACH CARD YOU WILL NEED:

- One 5¾ inch x 8½ inch sheet of thin black card
- One 8½ inch x 11 inch photocopied sheet of music
- A 8½ inch x 11 inch sheet of onion skin or similarly textured fine paper
- 16 inches narrow silver ribbon
- Silver sealing wax
- Ruler
- Craft knife
- Paper glue (spray adhesive works well)
- Typewriter or fine-nibbed pen
- Paper punch
- Silver marker pen
- Ring, coin or embossed button

1. *First fold the black card in half. To do this neatly, measure exactly where the center line lies and run a craft knife very lightly along this line. The knife must just score the surface of the card – take care not to cut through it. Fold the card then open it out flat again.*

2. *Apply paper glue or spray adhesive to the side of the card with the score line, and stick it to the back of the sheet of music-printed paper. Carefully cut off the excess paper around the card with a craft knife* (PHOTO 1).

3. *Fold the sheet of onion skin paper in half and trim ¾ inch off the length and width of the folded rectangle. Type the wording of your invitation on the inner right-hand side, or use a fine-nibbed pen to write it out neatly.*

4. *Position the folded paper inside the card* (PHOTO 2). *Punch two holes in the spine through both outer and inner components, then thread a length of silver ribbon through the holes and tie it in a decorative bow.*

5. *When sending out the invitations, address the envelopes with a silver marker pen and seal the flaps with silver sealing wax. If you don't have a seal, use a ring, coin or embossed button to make an impression in the sealing wax.*

The candle holders

Place an arrangement of candles at the center of the table and a single candle between pairs of place settings to create a magical atmosphere.

MATERIALS & EQUIPMENT

◆ White plastic plant pots — a large one for the center of the table and small ones for single candles
◆ Masking tape
◆ A block of styrofoam
◆ Sand

◆ An 8½ inch x 11 inch and a few 11½ inch x 17 inch photocopied sheets of music
◆ Double-sided tape
◆ Silver ribbon
◆ Large and small white candles

1. *Cover the hole at the bottom of each plant pot with masking tape. Wedge a block of styrofoam into the larger pot, making sure that it does not protrude above the top. (This will ensure that the pot does not become too heavy.) Pour sand over the styrofoam to cover it and to fill up any gaps in the pot. Fill the small pots with sand.*

2. *Stand each pot on the reverse side of a piece of photocopied paper in the middle of the sheet. Draw the paper up around the sides, holding it in place as you work with pieces of double-sided tape (PHOTO 1). When the paper is in place, wrap a ribbon around the top of the pot and tie the ends into a bow. Fan the edges of the paper out above the top of the pot. If the paper is not large enough to cover the plant pot generously, join two pieces together with adhesive tape on the reverse side.*

3. *Insert a group of white candles into the large pot, wedging them in the sand. A single smaller candle will suffice for each of the small pots.*

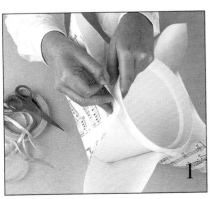

The napkins

Here is a very simple idea that will turn plain white napkins into a special and elegant finishing touch.

For each place setting, lay a napkin flat on the table, then fold it in half diagonally to form a large triangle. Roll this triangle up from the base to the point, and tie the roll into a loose knot. Before tightening the knot, insert the stem of a flower into the middle. Lay a napkin-wrapped flower on a plate at each place setting.

The place cards and menus

Personalized place cards on the table will show guests how much thought you have put into making them feel welcome. The method shown here involves printing each guest's name on a small piece of paper and inserting it into a decorated card with an attractive cut-out detail. The menus are created in a similar way, but the design is somewhat simplified.

MATERIALS & EQUIPMENT

◆ Thin black card
◆ Photocopied sheet music
◆ White paper
◆ 12 inches narrow silver ribbon for each place card or 16 inches for each menu
◆ Tracing paper, pencil and ruler
◆ Craft knife
◆ Paper glue or spray adhesive
◆ Typewriter, word processor, or fine-nibbed pen
◆ Paper punch

THE PLACE CARDS

1. *Trace* TEMPLATE 7.1 *on* PAGE 90 *onto a piece of tracing paper.*

2. *Cut out a 4-inch square from the black card. Apply paper glue or spray adhesive to the card and stick the card to the back of the music paper. Trim any excess music paper around the card with a craft knife.*

3. *Transfer the design you have traced onto the music-printed side of the card. Lightly score along the score lines (the dotted lines on the template on* PAGE 90).

2 inches

4 inches

⅜ inch

DIAGRAM 1

4. *Carefully cut along the lines of the design with a craft knife, then fold the card along the score lines so that the design stands up.*

5. *Cut a rectangle 2¾ inches x ¾ inch in size from the white paper. Type a guest's name across the piece of paper with a typewriter or a word processor, or write it out neatly with a fine-nibbed pen or silver marker pen.*

6. *Cut out a piece of black card, 3¼ inches x 1¼ inches in size. Stick the name to the center.*

MENU
Avocado Mousse

Grilled salmon
Baby potatoes
Minted peas
Greek salad

ELAINE

LAUREN

7. *Flatten the cut-out card, then draw a rectangle, 3¼ inches x 1¼ inches in size and 1 cm (⅜ in) in from the three edges, on the plain side of the half that will be the front of the finished card (DIAGRAM 1).*

8. *Mark points on each line ⅜ inch from the corners. Draw a diagonal line across each corner connecting these points, and cut along the diagonal lines with a sharp craft knife (DIAGRAM 1). Insert the corners of one of the printed cards into these slits (PHOTO 1).*

9. *Thread a ribbon through the stand-up design and tie the ends into a neat bow.*

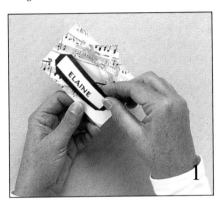

THE MENUS

1. *Cut the sheet of black card in half lengthwise to make two menus. Lightly score a line across the middle of each card with a craft knife.*

2. *Stick music paper onto the side with the score line, then trim any excess. Fold the card along the score line.*

3. *Print your menu on a piece of white paper 3¾ inches x 2¾ inches in size, and stick it onto a 4¼ inch x 3¼ inch piece of black card.*

4. *Mark the folded card and cut slits in it as you did in STEPS 7 and 8 of the namecards. Insert the corners of the printed menu in the slits.*

5. *Punch two holes just below the folded top edge of the menu, thread a ribbon through them and tie the ends into a bow.*

Little boxes

Give guests an inexpensive gift such as sugared almonds or a couple of homemade chocolates in a special box that they can take home as a memento of a special evening. Place the boxes on the table next to each place card. Here are two designs for you to choose from.

MATERIALS & EQUIPMENT

◆ One 8½ inch x 11 inch sheet of thick card for BOX A, or one 11½ inch x 17 inch sheet for BOX B
◆ One 8½ inch x 11 inch sheet of thin white card for BOX A, or one 11½ inch x 17 inch sheet for BOX B
◆ One 8½ inch x 11 inch photocopied music for BOX A, or one 11½ inch x 17 inch sheet for BOX B
◆ ¾ yards narrow silver ribbon for BOX A, or 12 inches for BOX B
◆ Tracing paper and pencil
◆ Craft knife
◆ Ruler
◆ Paper glue or spray adhesive

1. *Enlarge the design of BOX A on PAGE 90 or BOX B on PAGE 91 by 141% on a photocopier. Transfer the shape onto the thick card, and cut it out with a craft knife. Use this as a template to mark out the boxes on thin card*

(PHOTO 1). Carefully score along the fold lines (indicated on the template with dotted lines) with a craft knife, ensuring that you don't cut through the card. Cut out the shape of the box.

2. *Apply paper glue or spray adhesive to the side of the card with the score lines (PHOTO 2), and stick the card to the back of the sheet of music-printed paper. Use a craft knife to cut off the excess paper around the box shape.*

3. *Make up the boxes by folding along the score lines (PHOTO 3) and gluing if necessary. Insert your gift, and tie with a ribbon (see opposite page).*

CHAPTER EIGHT

Dinner by candlelight

Weave a secret message of love into a clever heart-shaped card to set the scene
for a romantic Valentine's Day dinner. Follow through with red roses wrapped in
tulle, color-coordinated tablemats and cloth napkins, and heart-painted champagne
glasses and candle shades. Stay with the traditional red and white,
and add the occasional accent of gold for a special touch.

The tablecloth

Loosely cover a tablecloth with a layer of white tulle.
You can play it safe with the ever-romantic white on white, or
try a traditional Valentine red on white or white on red. Scatter
red rose petals between the folds of tulle.

Painted glasses

Propose a toast to your loved one with these elegant, hand-painted glasses.

MATERIALS & EQUIPMENT

- ◆ Champagne glasses
- ◆ Gold glass paint
- ◆ Red glass paint
- ◆ Tracing paper and pencil
- ◆ Adhesive tape
- ◆ A fine paintbrush

1. *Trace the heart and swirl design on* PAGE 92 (TEMPLATE 8.2) *onto a small piece of tracing paper, then tape it in position inside the glass* (PHOTO 1).

2. *Paint in the swirls and the outline of the heart with the gold paint. When it is dry, paint the heart in red* (PHOTO 2).

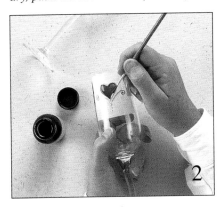

The napkins

Smart white napkins with a red border and back are given a whimsical finish by the addition of four heart-shaped red buttons. As they are decorative in themselves, the napkins can simply be folded in quarters and placed on a side-plate.

MATERIALS & EQUIPMENT

FOR EACH NAPKIN YOU WILL NEED:

- ◆ A 16-inch square of red cotton fabric
- ◆ A 14-inch square of white cotton fabric
- ◆ Red and white sewing thread
- ◆ Four red, heart-shaped buttons (if you can't find heart-shaped ones, use round ones)
- ◆ Tape measure
- ◆ Sewing machine
- ◆ Iron
- ◆ Scissors
- ◆ Tailor's chalk or a water-soluble fabric marker pen
- ◆ Pins

1. *Make up a 14-inch square red napkin by sewing a 1-inch hem all round the red fabric.*

2. *Press a 1-inch hem all round the white fabric, but do not stitch. Trim the folded hem to ¼ inch.*

3. *Measure 1 inch in from all four edges of the red square and mark out this inner square with tailor's chalk or a fabric marker pen. Pin the white fabric to the red, using the marked lines as a guide* (PHOTO 1).

4. *Feed white thread through the needle of a sewing machine and fill the bobbin with red thread. Stitch the white square to the red square just inside the edge of the white fabric. If your sewing machine's tension is correctly set, the stitching lines will be almost invisible, with white stitches on the white fabric and red stitches on the red fabric.*

5. *Find the center of the napkin by folding it into quarters. Using red thread, stitch four small, red buttons around the center on the creases* (PHOTO 2). *Apart from adding a decorative touch, the buttons will secure the red and white sections of the napkin to each other.*

The tablemats

Easy to make, these mats consist of a pretty paper doily stuck down onto a red cardboard or plywood base. If you wish to varnish the mats, be sure to use good-quality doilies and a spray varnish.

MATERIALS & EQUIPMENT

FOR EACH MAT YOU WILL NEED:

◆ Thick cardboard or thin plywood, cut into a circle 13 inches in diameter
◆ Red acrylic paint or a piece of red card at least 13 inches square
◆ A good-quality round, white, paper doily, 8-10 inches in diameter
◆ Spray adhesive
◆ Craft knife (if red card is used)

1. *Paint one side of each cardboard or plywood circle with two coats of red acrylic paint, and allow this to dry between coats. Alternatively, spray adhesive on the red card, stick it to the circle and trim the edges.*

2. *Apply spray adhesive to the backs of the doilies. Carefully position* *them in the center of the red circles and stick them down.*

NOTE: Coasters for glasses can be made in the same way, using small cocktail-size doilies stuck onto cardboard circles with a diameter 1¼ inches greater than that of the doilies.

Cards of love

The cards consist of two pieces interwoven to form a heart shape. They can be purely decorative, or you can conceal a short message of love within the woven strips. For an interesting texture, try using handmade paper.

MATERIALS & EQUIPMENT

◆ A sheet each of firm red and white paper
◆ 8 inches gold or white ribbon
◆ 110 inches x 20 inches white tulle (optional)
◆ Pencil and ruler
◆ Sharp scissors or a craft knife
◆ A fine-nibbed pen or calligraphy pen
◆ Hole punch

1. *Following* TEMPLATE 8.1 *on* PAGE 92, *mark out one half of the card on each sheet of paper. You can scale the size up or down to suit your requirements – if you work according to the template, the finished heart will be about 5 inches across and be made of ⅜-inch squares; larger ¾-inch squares will make an 8-inch heart. Cut out the shape with scissors or a craft knife.*

1

2. *Measure and draw the cutting lines from the bottom (straight) edge to points in line with the start of the curve, as shown in the template. Carefully cut along these lines* (PHOTO 1).

3. *Lay the pieces of paper at right angles to one another and weave the strips in and out to form the checked heart* (PHOTO 2).

4. *To plan your secret message, lightly mark on the white card with a pencil where the strips overlap and pull the two halves apart again. Write your message in the marked areas* (PHOTO 3) *and then reweave the heart to conceal it.*

5. *Although the card will hold together without it, a ribbon adds a decorative touch and also enables the heart to be*

hung. Punch a hole through both pieces of paper just below the right angle at the top of the heart. Fold the ribbon in half, thread the loop through the hole and secure the ribbon by pulling the cut ends of the ribbon through the loop (PHOTO 4).

6. *If you wish, tie a large tulle bow around the backs of both chairs and hang a heart from the center of each.*

The floral arrangement

Long-stemmed red roses are the essence of romance. Instead of the usual arrangement in a vase, though, these roses are set in a shallow container and held together by a large, white tulle bow, to coordinate with the tablecloth and chairs.

1. Cut the oasis down to size with a serrated knife to make it fit snugly into the basket or container.

2. Strip the rose stems of all their leaves except those just below the flowers. Carefully lay the flowers out in a row on your working surface and trim the stems with scissors so that they are all the same length.

3. Insert the roses into the oasis one at a time, so that they stand upright (PHOTO 1). Start at the center and work outwards until the oasis is well covered and the arrangement full.

4. Wrap the piece of tulle around the stems (PHOTO 2) and tie the ends into a large bow.

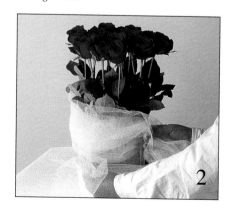

MATERIALS & EQUIPMENT

- ◆ Oasis
- ◆ A small, shallow, white basket lined with plastic, or a porcelain container such as a casserole, about 8 inches in diameter
- ◆ 20 straight-stemmed red roses
- ◆ 110 inches x 20 inches white tulle
- ◆ A serrated knife
- ◆ Scissors

The candleholders and shades

Turn the lights down low and let candlelight create the romantic atmosphere needed for a special Valentine's Day dinner. A glass lampshade is easily converted into a candleholder with a base made of play dough.

MATERIALS & EQUIPMENT

FOR THE SHADE YOU WILL NEED:

◆ A glass lampshade
◆ Gold glass paint
◆ Red glass paint
◆ Tracing paper and pencil
◆ Adhesive tape
◆ A fine paintbrush

FOR THE BASE YOU WILL NEED:

◆ 1 cup flour
◆ ½ cup salt
◆ 2 teaspoons cream of tartar
◆ 1 tablespoon cooking oil
◆ 1 cup boiling water
◆ Gold spray paint
◆ Red heart-shaped beads or rhinestones
◆ A saucer
◆ Clear adhesive glue

1. *Paint the glass lampshade, following the instructions given on* PAGE 67 *for the champagne glasses. Repeat the heart motif* (TEMPLATE 8.2 *on* PAGE 92) *at random over the entire surface, leaving off the swirls, and paint a ring of gold dots around the wide opening of the shade.*

2. *To form the base, mix the flour, salt, cream of tartar, oil and boiling water together to form a smooth dough. Although the dough will harden within a matter of hours, it should remain reasonably pliable for a few weeks if kept in an airtight container. Fill the saucer with the dough, pushing it down*

and smoothing over the top until it is level (PHOTO 1). *Leave the dough for a couple of hours to harden.*

3. *Gently ease the dough from the saucer and turn it onto its flat side. Mark the center point – just a visual estimate will suffice. Using the edge of the small opening on the glass shade, cut a hole in the center so that there is a circular support exactly the right size for the shade* (PHOTO 2). *Leave the dough in a warm, dry place to harden further.*

4. *Spray the dough base with gold spray paint. When the paint is dry, stick beads or rhinestones around the base with clear adhesive glue* (PHOTO 3).

5. *Stand the glass shade in the base and place a tall, red candle in the center.*

CHAPTER NINE

Christmas dinner

Take a break from the traditional colors of Christmas and deck out the table in crisp white with a sprinkling of golden stars and leaves. And don't pack away these decorations immediately after Christmas — they are sure to turn any meal into a special occasion.

Starry cloth and napkins

Spread a galaxy of stars across your dining table with this gold-printed, snowy white cloth, and echo the theme at each table setting with a starry napkin.

M A T E R I A L S & E Q U I P M E N T

◆ White tablecloth
(If you do not have a tablecloth, refer to *The basic cloth* on page 11
for instructions on how to make your own)
◆ Napkins
◆ Gold fabric paint
◆ Tracing paper and pencil
◆ A large, firm potato
◆ A sharp knife

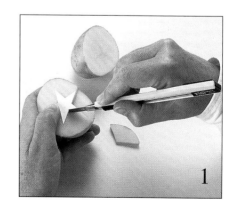

1. *Trace the larger star design on* PAGE *92; cut out the shape. Cut the potato in half and position the template on the cut surface. Carefully cut around the design with a knife, so that the star stands out by about ¼ inch* (PHOTO 1).

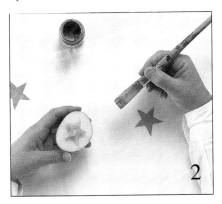

2. *Practise printing on a piece of scrap fabric before working on your cloth. Mix the fabric paint well, then apply it to the potato with a paintbrush* (PHOTO 2) *and press the potato down onto the scrap of fabric. Fresh paint must be applied after each print. When you are satisfied with the results, start printing the stars onto your cloth. A random sprinkling of stars is very effective, but if you wish to achieve a more formal look, mark out the position of the stars before starting.*

3. *Cut a smaller star on the other half of the potato and print the napkins in the same way.*

4. *Set your iron at the maximum temperature suggested for the material and iron on the reverse side of the cloth to fix the paint, going over each star for about three minutes* (PHOTO 3).

The napkin rings

These golden cherubs, made from molded plaster of Paris, are a perfect addition to your Christmas table setting.

MATERIALS & EQUIPMENT

◆ Molding plaster, such as plaster of Paris
◆ Large, brass curtain rings
◆ Gold spray paint
◆ A mold – the kind used
for molding chocolates works well

1. *Mix molding plaster with water until it has a custard-like consistency. Fill the mold and insert a curtain ring so that the join is just below the surface* (PHOTO 1). *You will have to support the ring for a few minutes until the plaster starts to harden.*

2. *When the plaster is hard — after about 15 minutes — carefully ease it out of the mold and leave it in a warm place to dry out completely.*

3. *Spray the front and back of the napkin ring with gold paint* (PHOTO 2).

The chargers

These golden, leaf-rimmed chargers are not meant to function as tablemats,
but rather as decorative frames for the dinner plates.

MATERIALS & EQUIPMENT

FOR EACH UNDERPLATE YOU WILL NEED:

◆ Several ivy leaves

◆ A square of thick cardboard at least 10 inches across

◆ Contact adhesive

◆ Gold spray paint

◆ Absorbent paper

◆ A pair of compasses

1. *As the leaves must be pressed, you will need to prepare them several days in advance. Place them between sheets of absorbent paper in thick books, ensuring that the leaves do not overlap each other (PHOTO 1). After a few days they should be nice and flat.*

2. *Draw a circle about 10 inches in diameter on the cardboard and cut it out carefully with a craft knife.*

3. *Lay the leaves loosely on the edge of the cardboard circle so that they overlap each other and conceal the cardboard*

circle's edge. When you are happy with the arrangement, stick the leaves one by one to the cardboard (PHOTO 2).

4. *When the glue has set, spray the cardboard and leaves with a good coat of gold paint (PHOTO 3).*

Christmas crackers

Christmas crackers add a special touch to any Christmas party. Make your own to match your gold and white table setting, and choose a special little gift to insert for each person at the meal.

MATERIALS & EQUIPMENT

FOR EACH CRACKER
YOU WILL NEED:

◆ A piece of firm white paper
(not too thick) or starry
wrapping paper, measuring
7 inches x 14 inches
◆ Three pieces of thin card for
the inner tubes, each measuring
3¼ inches x 6 inches
◆ Thin cord or ribbon
◆ Paper glue or
double-sided tape
◆ Self-adhesive stars for decoration
(if plain paper is used)
◆ A small gift
◆ A cracker pull (if available)

1. *Roll up the three pieces of card for the inner tubes to a diameter of 2 inches. Overlap the ends and stick them together with tape or glue.*

2. *Stick the three tubes along the bottom edge of the paper rectangle, with the middle tube centered and the outer tubes ⅝ inch in from either side of the paper (PHOTO 1). Insert a gift and cracker pull. Roll the paper*

tightly around the card tubes and secure the overlapping edge with glue or small pieces of double-sided tape.

3. *Tie a piece of cord or ribbon between the central and outer cores and squeeze gently, taking care not to tear the paper (PHOTO 2). Repeat for the other end. Decorate the cracker with self-adhesive stars if desired.*

Topiary tree

There are two ways to prepare a "topiary tree" centerpiece. The first is to plant ivy in a pot and train it around a wire shape. The disadvantage of this method is that you will need literally months to achieve the desired effect; on the other hand, you will have a permanent "tree" which, if properly trimmed, will look good for years. The second, "instant" method, shown here, involves winding cuttings of trailing ivy around a wire shape. Of course, the ivy will start to wilt after a day or two, so the "tree" should be prepared on the day you want to use it.

MATERIALS & EQUIPMENT

- ◆ White crepe paper
- ◆ Plastic plant pot
- ◆ Masking tape
- ◆ Gold ribbon
- ◆ Potting soil
- ◆ Wire that is sturdy yet pliable (a wire coat hanger is ideal)
- ◆ Ivy plant or ivy cuttings
- ◆ Pebbles or small styrofoam balls
- ◆ Gold spray paint (optional)

1. *Pleat a length of crepe paper and use it to cover the pot* (PHOTO 1). *Secure the paper to the bottom and inside of the pot with masking tape. Wrap a length of ribbon around the neck of the pot and tie the ends in a bow. Fill the pot with soil.*

2. *Bend the wire into the shape of your choice. You may choose to stick to the conventional Christmas tree shape, or try a heart, star or circle. Leave a long, straight piece at the base to anchor the wire. Insert this into the soil and make sure that the structure is sturdy.*

3. *If you are following the first method mentioned, plant the ivy in the pot and wind the stem around the wire; as the plant grows, gently train it to follow the shape of the wire. If you are taking the "instant tree" route, simply twist lengths of ivy around the wire until you have a well-covered, bushy effect* (PHOTO 2).

4. *Cover the soil with pebbles, or with small polystyrene balls or chips that have been sprayed with gold paint.*

Decorated candles and leafy wreath

A handful of gold pins will transform plain white candles into elegant table decorations. Make your design as simple or as complex as you like, and if you like an ornate or colorful effect, try using sequins instead of pins.

MATERIALS & EQUIPMENT

◆ White candles in a range of sizes
◆ Gold map tacks, or gold sequins or beads and short pins
◆ Thick wire (such as a coat hanger)
◆ Fronds of ivy
◆ Gold spray paint
◆ White plate
◆ Paper, ruler and pencil
◆ Adhesive tape

1. *Measure the height of each candle. Cut strips of paper as wide as each candle is high. Wrap a strip of paper around each candle and draw a pencil line to mark the overlap. Remove the paper from the candle and cut along the pencil line. The paper should now fit around the candle exactly.*

2. *Lay the paper flat and draw a design to indicate the positioning of the tacks or sequins. You may wish to create a grid for a geometric arrangement, or draw a shape such as a star.*

3. *When you are happy with your design, wrap the paper around the candle and hold it in place with a piece of tape. Push map tacks into the candle on the marked points shown on the paper or, if you are using sequins or beads, insert a straight pin through the center of each sequin or bead and into the candle (PHOTO 1).*

4. *When you have studded all the points, carefully tear away the paper (PHOTO 2).*

5. *To make the wreath, bend the wire to form a circle just smaller than the plate, twist lengths of ivy round the*

wire until it is well covered (as for the Topiary tree, opposite), then spray the wreath with gold paint.

6. *Group the candles on a white plate and position the gold-leafed wreath around them.*

CHAPTER TEN

Child's play

For a tiny tot's birthday party, you can't beat a really bright table setting.
Put your child to work to devise a vibrant "show of hands" with a tablecloth that
is literally hand-painted. Then turn sheets of colored card into masks, little boxes to
fill with candy, and embellishments for the straws, and finally
construct a balloon-filled centerpiece for a real lift-off.

The tablecloth

Prints made by hands dipped in paints of various colors create wonderfully spontaneous designs that will delight the little ones. If you don't have a cloth that you are happy to paint on, use an old sheet or make a cloth out of the cheapest fabric you can find. Refer to *The basic cloth* on page 11 for instructions on how to make a square, rectangular or round tablecloth.

MATERIALS & EQUIPMENT

APART FROM A PAIR OF EAGER LITTLE HANDS, YOU WILL NEED:

◆ A white cotton cloth
◆ Fabric paint in an assortment of bright colors
◆ Glass jars or foil baking trays (one for each color of paint)
◆ Newsprint
◆ A large paintbrush
◆ Permanent black fabric marker pen

1. Pour a small quantity of fabric paint into separate jars or foil trays. If the paint is too thick, use water to thin it down to the consistency of cream. Prepare all the colors, even though you will work with only one at a time.

2. It is a good idea to practice the printing on a scrap of fabric first in order to establish just how much paint and pressure is required to produce a pleasing print. Cover a large, flat surface with newsprint and lay the scrap fabric on top of it. Starting with one color, dip the paintbrush into one of the jars of paint and apply a coat to the palm and fingers of your child's hand (PHOTO 1).

The hand is then pressed onto the cloth to transfer the paint. You will need to reapply the paint after each impression and keep each coat of paint as thin as

1

possible — if you try to save time by applying a thick coat or dipping the hands into the paint to make a few impressions before having to reapply, you will probably end up with some very blurred and blotchy prints

3. When you and your child have mastered the technique, spread the cloth onto the newspapers and start printing. Space the prints far apart in a random fashion, until you are satisfied that there is adequate coverage of the first color on the entire cloth (PHOTO 2).

4. Wash the paintbrush and your child's hands well before proceeding with the next color. Continue working through all the colors until the cloth is well covered.

5. When the paint is completely dry, press the cloth on the reverse side with a very hot iron to fix the paint.

6. Finally, use a black fabric marker to draw dots for eyes and a curved line for a smiling mouth on the palm of each printed hand (PHOTO 3).

The straws

Hold hands and smile... then follow the theme of the tablecloth with these delightful junior "cocktail" straws. The hands are simply cut from colored card and wrapped around flexible straws.

MATERIALS & EQUIPMENT

- ◆ Colored card to match the handprints on the tablecloth
- ◆ Flexible plastic drinking straws
- ◆ Tracing paper and a pencil
- ◆ Scissors or a craft knife
- ◆ Black felt-tipped pen
- ◆ Double-sided tape

1. *Trace the hand design on* PAGE 93 *and transfer it onto the colored card, making a pair of hands for each straw.*

2. *Cut out the shapes, cut two slits as indicated, and draw in a pair of eyes and a mouth on the palms of the hands with a black pen, as for the tablecloth.*

3. *Take each pair of hands and stick a small piece of double-sided tape onto the strip of paper between the two hands. This will hold the card in place. Wrap each pair of hands around a straw and slide the two small slits into one another to join the hands together.*

The dice

Many children's games involve throwing dice. Give each child a giant dice that is actually a box
filled with sweets. You could even devise a couple of games that involve playing with the dice during the party.
Although those shown here have been made from colored card, you could opt for the more
traditional — and dramatic — black cube with white spots.

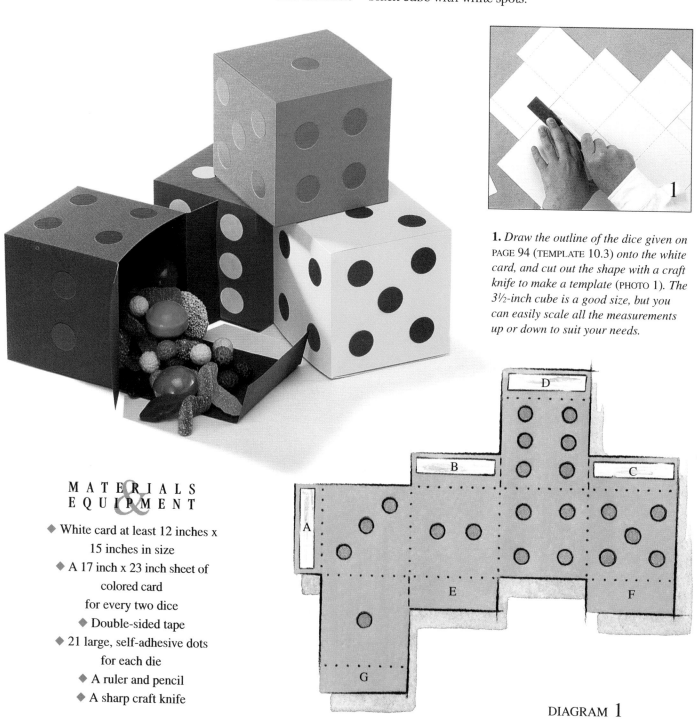

1. *Draw the outline of the dice given on*
PAGE 94 (TEMPLATE 10.3) *onto the white
card, and cut out the shape with a craft
knife to make a template* (PHOTO 1). *The
3½-inch cube is a good size, but you
can easily scale all the measurements
up or down to suit your needs.*

MATERIALS & EQUIPMENT

◆ White card at least 12 inches x
15 inches in size

◆ A 17 inch x 23 inch sheet of
colored card
for every two dice

◆ Double-sided tape

◆ 21 large, self-adhesive dots
for each die

◆ A ruler and pencil

◆ A sharp craft knife

DIAGRAM 1

2. *Use the template to mark out all the boxes on the colored card, and cut them out with a craft knife.*

3. *Score all the fold lines by lightly running the blade of your craft knife along them. Take care not to cut all the way through the card.*

4. *Mark out the position of the dots on the same side as the score lines, as indicated on* DIAGRAM 1, *and stick the self-adhesive dots in place* (PHOTO 2).

5. *Stick a strip of double-sided tape on flap A as indicated on* DIAGRAM 1. *Start making up the boxes by folding along the scored lines and sticking flap A to the inside edge of the side with five dots on it* (PHOTO 3).

6. *Fold in flaps B and C and the side with six dots on it and stick them down. Then stick flap D to the inside of the side with three dots on it. Fill the box with sweets. Finally, fold in flaps E and F and close the lid (the side with one dot) by tucking flap G into the side marked with four dots.*

The masks

Turn colored card into fun masks by cutting out a basic shape and decorating it with bright self-adhesive dots. If you are feeling creative, design your own mask shape and adorn it with sequins, beads, ribbons and whatever other materials you think will look good.

MATERIALS & EQUIPMENT

◆ Colored card – you will need a rectangle about 8½ inches x 3 inches in size for each mask
◆ Colored self-adhesive dots
　◆ Hat elastic
　◆ Tracing paper or carbon paper
　◆ A pencil
　◆ Scissors and a sharp craft knife
◆ A darning needle or a sturdy cocktail stick

1. *Copy the mask shape given on* PAGE 93 (TEMPLATE 10.2), *reducing its size if necessary, and transfer it onto the piece of colored card using tracing paper or carbon paper. Alternatively, create your own designs and draw them onto the card.*

2. *Cut out the outline with scissors and the eye holes with a craft knife.*

3. *Decorate the mask with the self-adhesive dots.*

4. *Using a darning needle or cocktail stick, make a small hole on either side in line with the eyes. Thread a length of elastic through these holes and tie a knot at each hole to hold it in place.*

The centerpiece

A fountain of smiley-faced balloons and colored napkins spills out of a paper bag to create a bright and cheerful focal point to the party table. The paper bag featured here is relatively simple to make, and is also perfect for holding gifts — especially oddly shaped objects that are awkward to wrap. Just scale the measurements up or down to produce the appropriate size for your table centerpiece or for gifts.

MATERIALS & EQUIPMENT

- A 25 inch x 14 inch sheet of white card
- A small quantity of two of the paint colors used for printing the tablecloth
- Double-sided tape
- 7½ inch x 4 inch piece of stiff card
- 28 inches thin, brightly colored nylon or cotton rope
- Balloons in assorted colors — 10 for the centerpiece and 3 for the back of each chair
- String and/or balloon sticks
- Colored paper napkins
- Pencil and ruler
- A sharp craft knife
- A large paintbrush
- Paper punch
- A black felt-tipped pen
- Helium canister (if available)

1. *Lay the card on a flat surface. Mark out the score lines with a pencil and ruler (*SEE TEMPLATE 10.4 ON PAGE 95*). Run a craft knife lightly along these lines, scoring the dashed lines on the inside of the card and the dot-and-dash lines on the outside.*

2. *Fold over 1¼ inches along the top edge and ¾ inch along the left-hand edge towards the side of the card that will become the inside of the bag, as shown in the template.*

3. *Print two hands on the card as shown in* PHOTO 1, *using one color for each side and following the method used to print the tablecloth. Draw a smiling face on each handprint with a felt-tipped pen.*

4. *Stick the short edges of the bag together with double-sided tape. Stick a piece of double-sided tape along the inside bottom edge of the paper, as shown in the template and* PHOTO 2.

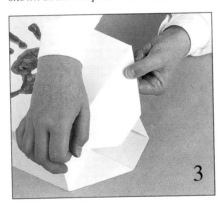

5. *Fold the card along the score lines so that the bag begins to take shape — as though you were wrapping a rectangular present (*PHOTO 3*).*

6. *Remove the backing from the double-sided tape and stick the bag together, then stick the piece of stiff card inside the bottom of the bag for stability.*

7. *Punch two holes for each handle along each of the bag's two long top edges.*

8. *Cut the length of rope in half. Thread each piece of rope through the punched holes and knot the ends on the inside so that handles are formed (*PHOTO 4*).*

9. *Inflate a batch of colorful balloons. If possible, fill them with helium so that they don't droop. (Helium canisters can be rented or you can buy ready-inflated balloons from a professional party planner.) Tie a length of string to each balloon. If you can't get hold of helium, fill the balloons with air and either use short pieces of string to prevent them from drooping, or attach the balloons to balloon sticks, which hold them upright. Use a black felt-tipped pen with a broad nib to draw a smiling face on each balloon.*

10. *Stand the completed bag in the center of the table. Place a heavy weight such as a thick book or half a brick in the bag. Anchor the strings of the balloons under the weight so that the balloons float about 12 inches above the top of the bag. Fill the opening of the bag with at least one paper napkin of each color. Lay each napkin out flat, then pinch it at the center point between a thumb and forefinger and use your other hand to flute it gently. Insert the center point into the bag so that the corners fan out prettily at the top (*PHOTO 5*).*

2 . 1

2 . 2

5 0 %

3 . 1

3 . 2

3 . 3

4 . 1

4 . 2

4 . 3

6 0 %

4 . 4

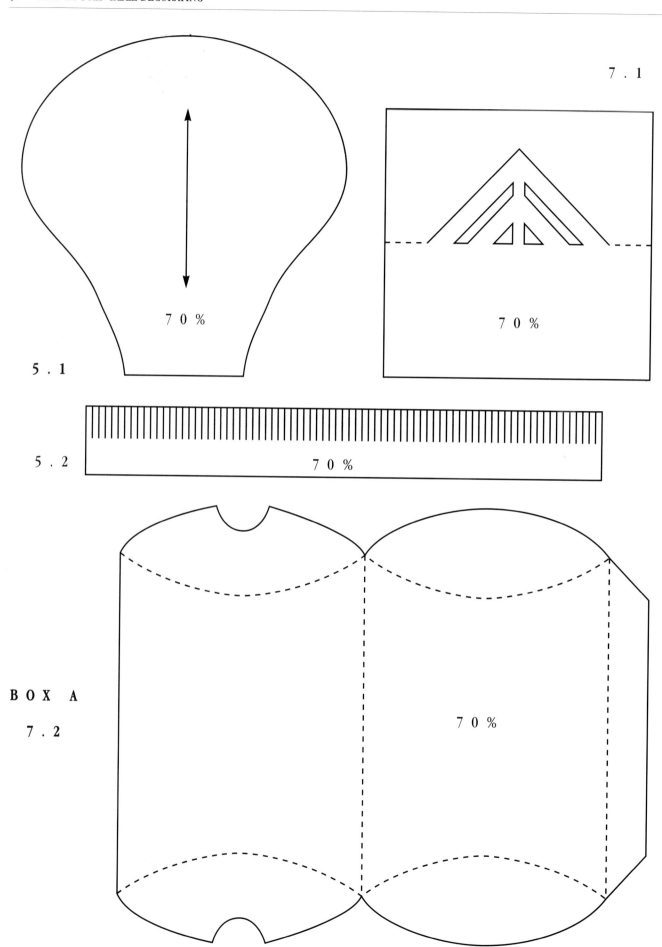

7 . 1

7 0 %

7 0 %

5 . 1

5 . 2   7 0 %

B O X   A

7 . 2   7 0 %

TEMPLATES • 91

70 %

BOX B

7 . 3

8 . 1

9 . 1

8 . 2

10.1

10.2

10.3

60%

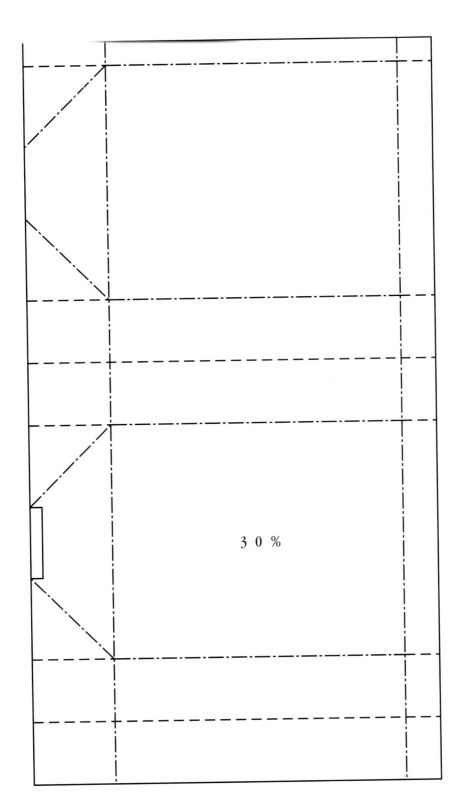

30 %

10 . 4

I N D E X

This edition published by Adams Media Corporation
260 Center St, Holbrook, MA 02343

EDITOR: Jenny Barrett
DESIGNER: Odette Marais
PHOTOGRAPHER: Juan Espi
STYLIST: Elaine Levitte
ILLUSTRATOR: Lara Volpert
TEMPLATE ILLUSTRATOR: Darren McLean

ISBN 1-58062-022-1 (p/b)

ACKNOWLEDGMENTS

I owe thanks to many people who helped to make this book possible — firstly, thanks to Ian, my family and friends for their support, and to Zoe Henshaw and Lauren Morris for helping to make the projects; thank you to Linda de Villiers of Struik Publishers for her encouragement and faith in me, and also at Struik, Jenny Barrett and Odette Marais for all their hard work; to Juan Espi for many patient hours behind the camera, and to Dudley Fillies for assisting. Lara Volpert, thank you for the beautiful illustrations. A special note of thanks to the following shops for the generous loan of accessories for the photographs: Mystique, Collector's Corner, Outdoor Lifestyle, Block and Chisel, Clarewood Antiques and Interiors, Boardmans, Stuttafords, Biggie Best (Claremont), Peter Visser Interiors, The Yellow Door and The Fresh Flower Company. A big thank you to Belinda Wilkinson of Chinaworks for her lovely hand-painted plates that inspired the projects in the 'Bright for breakfast' chapter. And last but not least, I must mention my dog and cats whose undemanding companionship means so much to me, and Alessi whom I will miss forever.

Printed and bound in Malaysia